THE STORY

THE STORY

In case of loss, Please return to: